ANIMAL FAMILIES / FAMILIAS DE ANIMALES

PENGUINS / PINGÜINOS
LIFE IN THE COLONY / VIDA EN LA COLONIA

Willow Clark Traducción al español: Eduardo Alamán

PowerKiDS press™

New York

Published in 2011 by The Rosen Publishing Group, Inc.
29 East 21st Street, New York, NY 10010

First Edition

Editor: Jennifer Way   Traducción al español: Eduardo Alamán
Book Design: Julio Gil

Photo Credits: Cover, back cover, pp. 9 (top left), 11 (top), 15, 20–21, 23, 24 (bottom right) Shutterstock.com; pp. 5, 6–7, 24 (top right) Tom Brakefield/Stockbyte/Thinkstock; pp. 8, 9 (top right, bottom right), 10–11 (main), 17, 19 iStockphoto/Thinkstock; p. 9 (bottom left) Jupiterimages/Photos.com/Thinkstock; pp.12–13, 24 (bottom left) David Tipling/Getty Images; p. 24 (top left) Doug Allan/Getty Images.

Library of Congress Cataloging-in-Publication Data
Clark, Willow.
[Penguins. Spanish & English]
Penguins = Pingüinos : life in the colony : vida en la colonia / by Willow Clark. — 1st ed.
    p. cm. — (Animal families = Familias de animales)
Includes index.
ISBN 978-1-4488-3124-1 (library binding)
1. Penguins—Juvenile literature. 2. Penguins—Life cycles—Juvenile literature. 3. Familial behavior in animals—Juvenile literature. I. Title. II. Title: Pingüinos.
QL696.S47C5318 2011
598.47—dc22
                                   2010025998

Manufactured in the United States of America

CPSIA Compliance Information: Batch #WW11PK: For Further Information contact Rosen Publishing, New York, New York at 1-800-237-9932

Web Sites: Due to the changing nature of Internet links, PowerKids Press has developed an online list of Web sites related to the subject of this book. This site is updated regularly. Please use this link to access the list:
www.powerkidslinks.com/afam/penguin/

CONTENTS

CONTENIDO

Penguins come together in a group called a **colony**.

Los pingüinos se reúnen en grupos llamados **colonias**.

A penguin colony meets up in the same place year after year.

Las colonias de pingüinos se reúnen en el mismo lugar todos los años.

7

There are 17 kinds of penguins. The emperor penguin is the largest penguin.

Existen 17 clases de pingüinos. El pingüino emperador es el pingüino más grande.

Gentoo Penguin
Pingüino papúa

8

Adélie Penguin

Pingüino de Adelia

Emperor Penguin

Pingüino emperador

Rockhopper Penguin

Pingüino de penacho
amarillo.

Chinstrap Penguin

Pingüino barbijo

9

The emperor penguin is the only animal that lives on Antarctica year-round.

El pingüino emperador es el único animal que vive el año entero en la Antártida.

Antarctica
——————
Antártida

11

Emperor penguins **huddle**. They take turns getting warm in the middle.

Los pingüinos emperador se **reúnen** en grupo. Toman turnos para calentarse en el centro del grupo.

Penguins find **mates** within their colony. The female penguin lays an egg.

Los pingüinos encuentran **parejas** en su colonia. Las pingüinas hembra ponen huevos.

14

Penguin parents take turns keeping the egg warm in their **brood pouches**.

Los pingüinos se turnan para mantener los huevos calientes. Los pingüinos **empollan** sus crías.

A chick comes out of the egg. Its parents hold the chick in their brood pouches.

Este polluelo sale del huevo. Sus padres lo mantienen caliente entre sus piernas.

18

The chicks huddle together while their parents look for food.

Los polluelos se quedan juntos mientras sus padres buscan la comida.

The chicks leave the colony to find their own food when they are older.

Cuando son más grandes, los polluelos salen de la colonia para buscar comida.

Words to Know / Palabras que debes saber

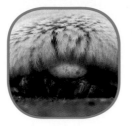

brood pouch / empollar

colony / (la) colonia

huddle / reunión

mates / (las) parejas